QUESTIONS FROM THE INTERIOR

ALSO BY SETH JANI

Let Us Rejoice: Poems 2003-2009

QUESTIONS FROM THE INTERIOR

POEMS BY
SETH JANI

SEVEN CIRCLEPRESS · SEATTLE, WA · 2014

Questions from the Interior by Seth Jani
2014 Seven CirclePress 1st Edition
ISBN-13: 978-0-615-78476-2

Published by Seven CirclePress: A Homegrown Literary Venue
Help Support Grassroots Literature Visit: www.sevencirclepress.com

Cover Painting: Cosmic Explosion by Ashley J. Velon
www.velonartwork.com

The author wishes to gratefully acknowledge the journals in which many of these poems first appeared:
Buddhist Poetry Review: "Each Thing in Turn," "Lessons from Dong Yuan," "Manifesto"
Camroc Press Review: "A Poem About Wind"
Shoots and Vines: " A Modern Death," "Aubade," "Bird," "Flight," "Metamorphosis," "Music," "Speech"
Writers' Bloc (Rutgers): "Jolt," "Travel Advertisement"
Foundling Review: "Voices"
tinfoildresses: Desert Snow

For AJ
Because the past had its purpose and its joy

TABLE OF CONTENTS

QUESTIONS FROM THE INTERIOR

SPEECH

Our words are rugged now;
Their grace flown suddenly out
Like sunlight in the evening,
Coarse replicas of the essential prayer
Latent in the heart of things.

Someday I want to come again
To the true, unspoken language,
Beyond semantics, where river does not mean
A simple swath of water
But a state of indescribable flowing.
Where our common tongue will be shared
With flowers, roots, and stars,
And our names signify
One anonymous center
Out of which
The world's music flows.

PERHAPS THAT'S WHY

No one is listening to the rain.
Its voice, like that of memory,
Cooling the summer trees.
And I come to ask
What place I have
In the beautiful clockwork of evening?

May I be stretched thin in the transparent light?
May I go down into the roots of things
And bury my head beneath the earth?

The world is our friend because it doesn't know
That we suffer,
That we are suffering.
The wind goes on revolving
Whether we regard its mindless tapping,
And there is no sadness in the night
Save that which our own heart
Wrings out in echoes.

The sky has no longing
To pour into poems,
And the earth knows nothing
Of love or death.
Perhaps that is why
In the gaze of speechless animals
We bow down like troubled children,
Clutching their softened bodies
Madly to our own.

A MODERN DEATH

And were you prepared to die?
Trapped inside that perfect scheme
Your reason painted?
The great white bird of your soul
Weighed down by your faith in gravity?
For you there was no other side,
No continuum.
Just a flash,
A steady trudge,
A flash,
Then nothing.
God was just a hermit's dream
And never that kernel inside yourself.
Life was just a waning light
And never luminosity.

THESE ARE THE REASONS

Because a verdict can never be reached,
Because the truth is not a stone
To be rolled gently in our hands,
To be inspected,
      weighed,
      written-out.
Because love is inseparable from sadness
And anger is only the fire of life   misinformed.
Because friendship is our longing for each other
And our inability to bypass the body.
Because what we want to say
Can never quite be said.
These are the reasons why I choose
Song instead of speech,
The dream of flying
Over the fact of flight.

METAMORPHOSIS

In the great and lonely light
I aim to waken,
Arms outstretched
With the weight
Of budding wings,
The curve of wind
Around my waist.
We do not dream
As an act against reality
But as a way of planting seeds.
To merely live is not enough,
Lift those arms in adulation!
Giving back to the world
The good, soft stuff of life.

SONG OF MY YOUTH

In every hour of your life
There is a certain kind of music,
A song that lies
Deep down
Hidden in the gruff
And that occasionally rises up
To dance beside you
As you fumble at the mirror
Or stand silent in the rain.

This song, like all great music,
Can only be heard at twilight,
When the houses grumble in their dreams
And the dog lies peacefully at the door.
In these moments you know you should be sleeping
But stand instead beside the window
Looking out upon the restful world
Thinking how you have finally found
Your one, true love.

JOLT

Longing is white like the wind
And it comes
Tearing up the house,
Overturning our perfect arrangements,
Sending its music
Straight into the heart
Of our stolid lives.

No window can shut out its coming.
No door can block its full advance.
It comes like a mythic apprehension,
Like a jolt
From the machinery of God.

Over the seamless threads of existence,
Over the seamless skeletons of dream,
It batters, burns and breaks,
Ripping out from inside our bodies
Our flimsy sense of self,
Leaving in its wake
A head full of fire.

FLIGHT

Love will pull us together.
In the dark I hasten after you,
Trying to lure creation with a prayer,
To rouse the wind
From a bed of leaves.

The imperishable is always with us
But the forms we secretly cherish
Drift off one by one,
And their reality becomes as questionable
As the handiwork of dreams.

Here, in this world that is not as solid as we believe,
Let me wrap my arms around the whirlwind,
Let me step into the dust-filled air,
My feet overwhelmed with flight
And treading not seconds, but eternities.

DURING RAIN

On an evening dark with rain
It seems inevitable
That sadness will get the best of us,
That our dreams will furl their wings
And softly refuse to fly,
That the sun which we trusted so carelessly
Will never emerge from its secret place
Of hiding,
That what we thought most holy
Will turn its head and prove a sham.

On these evenings I hold on
To what is most essential.
Grip a stone inside my palm
Or clutch a handful of the earth,
Pressing the heavy soil
Against my face,
Hoping to taste a hint
Of the world's intimacy.

In the night the leaves are stripped
Of their green pretensions
And they sway gently in the rain,
Urging us not to fight so blindly
And to hear
In the quiet moments of the day
Not a record of our failures
But that simple, stately music
Which underlies our every movement
And falls as lightly through our lives
As water through the trees.

DESERT SNOW

It's unexpected really,
Crawling out one morning
From the warm belly of sleep
To find the tent poles shaking around you,
To hear the breath
Of some mysterious stranger
Tapping at the door.
You unzip the weathered canvas
And step newborn into the light,
Dazzled how the expected waste
Has suddenly vanished
Leaving in its place
A world without roads.
You realize this is what we all await:
The day when the world will melt,
When the familiar scenes will disappear,
When you will step out from inside your house
To find that your footprints have been covered,
And that the places you've named and loved
Are shining before you
Beautifully unknown.

QUESTIONS FROM THE INTERIOR

Deep down where reason cannot reach
The curious in you begins to speak,
The true man with his soft, gray voice,
The true man with his penchant for mysteries.

The questions he has are not bred for logic.
They cannot be calculated or controlled.
They cannot be named, numbered, or announced.
They concern such things as the longing of the wind,
The insoluble riddle of the sea,
The moon, which shines so sadly
But never weeps.

They do not concern the "You" you think you are,
Or the "I" I think I am,
Not even the names we name the world.
They neither impart nor demonstrate,
Fill your head full of knowledge
Nor empty you to the core.

The true man, with his mouthful of questions,
Urges you only to ask:
How morning can come so softly
When the sun is so immense?
What is it that shines in sidewalks after rain?
What force really stops
A tear from lifting off the table,
Or a wounded heart
From breaking into song?

MUSIC

Today, I sit in the partial darkness
Softly stringing my instrument,
And bowing deep before the music
I await.

This is where it all begins;
Silence around my fingers,
The wind, all whispers, in my ears,
The grave internal beat
Continuously pounding.

Is this too where God began?
Not with smoke or fire,
Not with invectives or rage,
But with a slow hum inside
His heart?
A rustle, like wings arising?
An outcry, like the voice of joy?

And did he form in the metaphor
Of his mouth
That initial booming sound
Which spread its wings
And sailed down the centuries
Breaking here and there
Into the hands of Mozart?
Into Dylan's bleeding voice?
Into the sad, side-street sax?

The same sound that continues to sail
Right into my room
Where I sit
Piecing it together,
As though by grasping a single star
You could possibly understand
The mystery of light.

WE WILL CHANGE

I will change on a marvelous night
When the moon ripens in the sky
And the great plant of the Earth
Withdraws its emerald lids,
Lifting up its blossoms
In homage to the light.

The world too will change,
Not merely dust
But a place of blooming,
Its mountains and oceans
Shining in the dark,
A momentous tree
Spreading its luminous leaves
Out into the garden of Space.

We will change, and there will be
No more suffering,
Returned with our fumblings and rage
To the homeland of the Earth.
Our bodies finally recognized
For their spot amongst the animals,
With the neurons in the brain
Innumerable as galaxies,
And the heart, beating at the center,
Like a sea-dark star.

VOICES

So perfectly aligned and tender,
Those voices we hear daily from the sea
That could as easily belong to a dead man or bird
As to the sea itself.
We follow them down to the shore
Searching inside the ceramic shells
Scattered on the sand,
Looking between rocks,
In the keels of ships,
Even in our own hearts
With their blue horizons.

We dig up and dig down,
Build castles hoping to coax
Some grand inhabitant,
Stand on the fringes of the tide
Believing in the power between worlds.
But still, the sea continues to speak
And we do not know if it is a ghost or god,
Or even if we are listening
To our own precious world
Trying to greet us
With a song.

RESOLUTIONS

Winter is undeniable with its accusations,
A rupture in the perfect sunlight of summer,
Informing us we have squandered another season
Never working on ourselves.

To not so disappoint the earth,
A hard mother who scolds us in our ease.
To rise to the cosmic purity embedded in our bones
And flick off the awkward dance of the bashful.

To discover the life smuggled beneath the overcoats of
Our century
And rip the gray garters from around our bodies;
Our flawless fruit-flesh open to the sun.

To stand, silent and shimmering, in the rain
And lift our old, petty tenets up into the night,
Asking whatever forces brought us here
To burn our borders down.

TRAVEL ADVERTISEMENT

Walking through the cosmos
Tonight at 11 p.m.
We'll strap stars to our sneakers,
Tenderly acquaint
The awkward joints of our bodies
With dustless angel arms
And lift-off, clearheaded,
Into the night.

The road we take may seem familiar.
The dead walk it daily
And it runs through your dreams
Dotting that intricate country
With sure signs of travel.
The same road you wandered as a child,
Standing on its special surface
Lost but not alone.

Tonight we'll follow it through the layers
Of the world,
You and I and the treacherous dark
Dancing beyond boundaries,
Cradled in the hearts of planets,
Rushing past blazing clusters,
Following the crystal footprints of creation
Back to that bright beginning
From which we all once traveled
Before we ever knew directions
Or the purpose of goodbyes.

AUBADE

The frostbit morning appears between
The trees,
Sudden chinks in the dark
That rip the smooth exterior
On the great hide of night.

Lovingly, we displace our shadows,
Feed our silhouettes to the sun,
Walk inside our bodies
With a different grace.

At this hour the world makes a promise
And we are assured that nothing really ends,
That the night is merely preparation
For the circles of the sun
And we need only to lift our arms in wonder
And speak with quiet words
Of constant praise.

A POEM ABOUT WIND

I believe in the metaphor of wind,
The thought that we are circling through our lives
With the same quiet passion
That blows newsprint through the night,
With the same subtle violence
That makes the thrashing of the trees
A kind of music.

I imagine what peculiar lightness comes
After traveling for centuries across the sea,
Having picked clean the bones of mammoths,
Snuffed the first, feeble flames,
Seen generations
With all their precious battles
Reduced to rumor.

I dream of how I want my heart to be
Like those solar gusts shooting off the sun,
Unsettling satellites,
Lighting the wakes of comets,
Dancing across the distant north
As though it were a burning breath
From the bellows of the universe.

BIRD

He designed the heart to be a bird.
A simple specimen
Pumping song
Into the corners of the body.
The capillaries
A near match
To the rush of wings.

And when love breaks
Through the tender casing,
He meant each fiber to flutter
And beat,
As though it were suddenly preparing
To rupture the ribcage
And fly away.

EARLY ONE MORNING

You never really grasped it all.
Every morning when you awoke
And the world had changed a little
In your sleep,
You slid through the early light
Trying to understand
The flickering shapes of things.
"Something's different," you'd say,
Though the sea remained at your window
And the stars continued on their age-old
Journey through the dark.

Dreams, you thought, are not native here,
But come from that other world in your sleep
And they rise through your body
To dance and dissolve,
Leaving you, early one morning,
Love-struck and alone,
Having to recall
Again and again
The shifting meanings of your life.

COSMOLOGY

Perhaps one day you will exclaim
My life is a star,
A pale, flickering point
Turning in the night,
Each moment a peculiar spark
Lighting the dust.
And you will walk, with all your reasons,
To the sea,
With all your dreams and silent meanings.
And there, in the great expanse of sand,
You'll lower yourself beneath the water
Where the moon will see you shine.
And looking to her side
She will notice
The sudden closeness of the dark,
The sure proximity of fear.
Then reaching down with her frostbit fingers
She will fish you from the sea,
Carving out in the hell-bent cosmos
Whatever it is we mean by *home*.

A WALK IN FEBRUARY

No elegance tonight;
Just the bare-bodied trees
With their milky shadows,
And a lonely poem
That hasn't learned
The mechanics of flight.
I sway in my small dilemmas
Thankful to bear
My tiny portion of pain
While 14 billion years of combustion
Continue to flare overhead,
Leaving me consoled
Under the white rose
Of winter stars.

AT THE START OF SPRING

It enters through the cracks inside your life,
After twenty years, maybe thirty,
You begin to doubt whatever it is
You have become.
You step out and feel a terrible kinship
With the wind,
With the jostling leaves, and inconsistent rain.

You let go of your misconceptions,
Faithful to the power of the earth,
To the kingdom of nature
Which knows only
The constant flux of rivers,
The circling passage of the year,
The tiny acorn
Which, inconceivably, bursts above your head,
Now guarding you against the sunlight,
Now giving refuge
To the robin's pneumatic song.

THE HUNGRY GHOSTS

By the time we could remember
Where it was we wanted to go
The houses had already darkened
And the small ghosts of streetlamps
Littered the evening,
Leaving only the instinctual dance
Of shadows and trees.

We were alone in our sickness,
Unable to describe what it was
For which we waited.
The gardens of our neighbors
Bloomed without our knowing
And we could not hear
The singular creak
Of a door that nearly opened.

We waited, and the hour, already late,
Grew later.
Our faces changed
With the setting sun.
Our flesh melted
With the clock.
Somewhere in the midst
Of what we squandered
Our bodies gave way
To the daemonic longings
We had always mislabeled,
Calling them
Perverse, misdirected,
Dwarfs of temptation,
Inheritances of disfigured youth.
All the tiny quirks
We counted as disruptions
And that turned out
To be angels after all.

DAWN BREAK

I lean in my body towards
The tilting wind,
The black drip of dawn break
At my back,
The puncture wounds of stars
Seeping overhead.

The pain of morning signals
From the trees,
Little, flickering lights
Rupturing the boughs
While the drunkard music of birds
Begins to churn.

The night, to whom I never
Announce my name,
Slinks back.
And everything which I
Am too afraid to understand
Dances in its mystery,
Leaving me alone
With the baffling glow of grasses,
The early voice of the river,
The barest speech of awe.

MANTRA

In the old ashrams
Denial led out of the world.
The monks with their empty mouths proclaimed
"Not this, not that,"
And what remained
Was neither seed, nor fruit,
Nor flower,
But just the essence that
Is no essence,
The god whose bounty
Is none.
In this hour
When the rain
Strikes the window
Leaving a shining residue
On the darkened panes,
I cannot believe in anything
But the soaking earth.
Fearful for its inhabitants
I bow down to touch the soil
Muttering to myself
"Only this, only this."

INITIATION

That day the earth was black.
I felt nothing. Knew nothing.
My heart was a husk
And the brittle wind could not
Ease its aches.
I walked the streets of a town
That would never be my home again.
The storefronts did not close
But everything offered
Seemed merely tokens to the dust.
The lake did not dry
But—deep down—the fish
Whistled in their bones.

The sun seemed indifferent.
Its winter light
Cold and cracking
On the side of silent houses.
And everything I had
So warmly understood
Yawned and shuddered
Like an open wound.

Not the music of the Mother,
The eternity of stars and oceans,
Could save me then.
Heartless. Howling in the dark.
I ripped flowers from their lawns,
Weeping with their naked roots
Inside my mouth.

Storm clouds gathered in the sky
And I yelled "Death" to them.
Rain ravaged the night
And I screamed "The End."
And the moon, which had always promised resurrection,

Bowed down to offer
Just a saddened, speechless light.

WE ARE TOGETHER

This is the only dream:
The eonic song of evolution,
The creeping dignity of grass,
Our lives laid out
To the insoluble rhythm
Of the sea's ancestral rocking.
And every day awaiting the final pump
That will softly undo our bodies
Stitch by quiet stitch.

I love the mouth with its constant questions.
I love the mystery we cannot name.
On the loneliest rock
Spat out in cosmic space
We are together.
And the wind says to us
"My brothers and sisters."
And the darkness says to us
"My little, darling lights."

OPPORTUNITY

If you cannot remember who you are,
If your name has left
The familiar refuge of your mouth
And seems unfathomable,
Do not approach a mirror,
Do not look anxiously for your face
Or repeat your digits to a friend.
But find a pond, somewhere,
Where the moon has lent
Its silver milk.
Find a deep spot
In the rain-soaked wood,
And look into the tiny crystals
The puddles make.
Look into the delicate glasswork
Shining forth
From the dampened grass.
Say to the slow hum of evening light
"May I grow transparent?"
Say to the nourishing dark
"May I begin again?"

LESSONS FROM DONG YUAN

Silence must be learned.
Though it has nothing to do
With the sound waves in a room,
Or how many miles you have trekked
Across mountains and deserts
Looking for the boundary
Which no voice may cross.

Rather it is a music you must build,
A garden inside the constant city,
A slow laboring of faith.
And there may still be birds there,
Cars with troubled engines,
Old leftover loves that have fallen
On the stone to perish.

But what matters is the way
You let these things
Step one by one into your hearing.
Like those old Chinese paintings
In which the artist slowly dissolves;
His eyes turning to acorns,
His body, a darkened plain.
And in the middle
His heart becoming that emptiness
Which even after the painting is finished
Will continue to listen
For the simple footsteps
Of whatever is yet to come.

GIVING FACES TO THE WORLD

Water is made of intricate crystals
Dancing on the pinpoint of the unknown.
And the heart, despite its elaborate vessels,
Is still portrayed
As two burning apples
Coupled in blood.

Wherever we go the tinniest details
Breakdown into the immensities of art.
The ocean is not just a comet's blessing
But our own neglected depths.
And the sun, whom we forget to covet,
Is still the same old monarch of the sky.

Not to mention the night
Dotted here and there
By the liquid radiance of stars,
Gases constellated solely to hang
Their ancestral lanterns
Above an ever lonelier earth.

Even here in this empty lot
Between two decrepit buildings
I secretly believe the homeless to be saints.
And rustling, on hands and knees, across the lawn
I catch a cricket conquering a grass blade.
His small green hunger greater than my own.

RITUAL

The art of ecstasy
Must be learned
Slowly and without words.
A lover's dive
Into the unknown heights
Of the body's movements.
A renunciation
Of our fear
To break with gravity.

We must even let go
Of the familiar and beloved.
Forget our names and identities
And don the soiled garments
Of a drunkard in the streets.

Then even our sense
Of being in the world
Must disappear.
We must become
Circuitous as air,
Our lives violently simmered
And the perfected ash
Offered to the gulls.

RISING WITH THE LIGHT

The morning dampens on a road
You have no intentions to walk.
The long treacherous pavement
Catching here and there
The phosphorescent sun,
While the rain
With its miniature mirrors
Sizzles and steams
At the touch of its whitened fingers.
Nothing now but our hearts
With their punctured solace,
The body with frail, invisible wings
Beating at our backs,
And the coffee, whose ecstatic black elixir
Swims with tiny charges.
Each pivoting spark
Waiting to enter
The calm waters of our blood.

WHAT ISN'T SAID

Summer's genesis.
Two birds and little bread.
The iris with its
Cycloptic yellow eye
Rising and falling
By the water.
We know only the stories
That are spoken,
Though every detail
Has its history.
The wind has whittled
Pyramids to dust,
And the cedar remembers
The great snows that fell
Before our lives began.

BURDEN

The hinges of the heart
Pivot in darkness.
We have nowhere to go
Besides where the night
Swarms with the opulence
Of stars.
Whatever it is that makes us
Love a wounded world
It enters our lives
With a darkened grace.
Not a blessing, but a troubled gratitude
We must carry on in quiet.

PENITENCE

The small bird whose death I caused
Leapt one night into my dreams.
Its tiny eyes
Like two flaked charcoals
Bore that glazed perplexion
I've seen so often in the dead.

Perhaps it had come
From the dark trees of the other world,
The obsidian sky
Beneath the earth,
The nocturnal meadows
Of the soul.

Whatever it was that brought
It to return to me
The guilt was unimaginable.
Its phantom song
Entered through my body.
I held it weeping in my palm.

A STORY

Love is not the journey that I dreamed
At ten years old, stepping out the door
Believing a great red horse
Would be riding past,
And that on it I would hook
My blustering heart
And awkward elegance
And stride with valiant effort
To the stars.

Instead the rivers were too high to cross,
The stallion lost its way amongst the wood,
And high-overhead the trees thatched
A seamless night.
Lonely and more hungry than in love
I built a little fire in the dark
And forgetful of where it was
I meant to go,
I burned my passions for their light.

THE PLOTLINE

It's about how you left town
One night, when winter had barely
Whitened the roads,
How you flew, or maybe dreamt
Your way across the country,
Landing on a bright day in California,
Your heart suffering a 2000 mile sickness.

It's about how different you felt,
Though your body, your voice, your history
Remained the same,
About how you came to believe
In the holiness of travel,
The sure meaning of letting-go,
The endless distance around you.

It's about how you laid down, finally,
Beside the girl for whom you waited,
Her dark hair shining in your fingers,
Her tiny shoulders resting in your hands.
And how you understood that even amidst
The whirlwind
Fate and love are certain.

A COSMIC LOVE POEM

Somewhere I have made my home
In the neighborhoods of the night,

Have salted stars on dinner plates,
Pressed luminous wine to my lips,

Have lit cigarettes with only a spark
Of cosmic dust,

Have raised three toddler moons
Orbiting my body,

Have worked diligently
For comets and light,

Have loved what can only be loved
Darkly, in those spaces far from earth:

Endless expansion and contraction,
Black holes, silence, gravity's loosened chain.

SOMETHING YOU MAY NOT KNOW

Perhaps it was on a morning
When you had nowhere to go.
In procession
Your obligations
Dropped one by one
Into the light,
And as though a river
Had opened in your blood
You felt a coursing music begin to flow.
Maybe we live only to touch
A single joy
And in those moments
You can believe
That at bottom
The world is endlessly happy.
A weightless ribbon of song
Greets you as you slowly lift
Your body deeper into spring,
Until you can hear
The audible inching of bone,
Or the dew dripping off
A distant cedar.
Nothing, my friend, is as secret
As the perfection of the earth.
Though sometimes, if you step lightly enough,
You may hear the insects going graciously
About their tasks.
Their tiny humming lives saying from below
"All you need has been granted."
"There is nothing you must change."

A SCENE

The delicate, undivided curve
Of an apple knocked idly to the earth
By a lonely boy in passing.
He has nowhere to go
And wanders the slope
Calculating the angles of sunlight,
Mapping out worlds
Beneath the mushrooms and moss.
He does not speak, but listens.
Presses his ear to the ground
Waiting for the roots to grow.
Or maybe he is learning to decipher
The mountain's cryptic shadow,
Or feeling for the first time
That mysterious grownup longing
Which, still too large for his body,
Causes him to bow his head and shake.

PASSING THROUGH THE HOLY SLUM

She was perfect because she walked
Dragging one foot behind her,
And he, because impatience
Lifted his eyes deep into his brow.
That day I remembered nothing about
The evangelicals and their spotless paradise.
Though the pigeons with their lonely, ruffled gray
Dazzled me as they pecked amongst the gutters.
Whoever says there is nothing to love
In moss-eaten furniture
Has never pressed their body to the dust.
Whoever refuses the grace of creaking houses
Will never know how beautifully exposed
Is the spirit of dilapidation.
The old ones say coming to ourselves
Is a road we walk in tatters.
Though there is gold on every table
The zest of life is always poured
Into the poorest, least-assuming bowl.

ORTUS

We know he only wanders
In imaginal skies.

Few books reference his mythic passage.

He has been sought for centuries.

Though he dies and resurrects,
He is really one.

In history he is known by many names.

He is propelled by fire.

He carries inscriptions on his wings.

No one has ever seen his nest.

One eye is brighter than the sun,
The other, moon-dark.

Somewhere it is said:
Remedium irae et dolaris
(Whoever finds this bird will be cured of all suffering).

You may shoot three arrows at his body.

A single hit and he will guide you.

Miss three and you will miss your life.

You must not covet or cage him.

He is only a sign along the way.

EXPOSURE

For a long time I held onto every word.

Gathered your breath into a tiny book
Of prayer.

Drove myself wild
Counting the intricacies
Of our time together.

Drew tiny symbolic circles,
Mandalas,
Then tossed them all to the hungry water.

I sprouted wings
And touched the untroubled
Mouths of stars.

And still, your voice
Vaguely echoed in my mind,
Traveled through my nerve ends,
Cataclysmic, unrelenting.

The flawed ceramic of my heart
Prepared to crumble.
And I waited, one day at a time,
For love's molecular music
To let a single, creeping seam
Begin to show.

DREAM WORK

You wake easily these days,
The slightest momentum of wind,
One scraggily howl from the dog
Next door.
You travel the length of your dreams
Only to lose the crucial insight
To a June Bug's clattering music.
And you may never know what it was
You missed.
That weightless, misunderstood kingdom
Rarely presents a key,
Though you have been faithful for decades.
Each night regularly attending the ritual;
Teeth first, brush inside its case,
Small sips of jasmine tea,
Body prostrate on the bed.
Still you wait, hoping that one marvelous thing
Will be revealed,
That the pieces will fall conspicuously into place,
That those countless radiant riddles
Will finally be understood.

EVERYTHING AT WORK

No easy labor: this twisting, pluvial music
Of the sky.
It enters the garden. Leaves one clear streak
Across the stone,
Tips its elixir to the stilted root-balls.
No perishing today, just the continual thirst
Wedging up from the earth,
Taking one more moment into its veins.
Beside the spade, the holly's shining body
Lifting and swaying in the wind.
And there, unnoticed in the dark,
The nightcrawler's tiny gray caboose
Sliding its way across the soil,
Asking nothing for its work
Besides the perfect currency
Of a morning filled with rain.

A DREAM FROM CHILDHOOD

It went on for hours.
That dream, where the walls
Seemed far away,
Where the bunk stretched
Miles above the carpet
With cold, vacuous space
Revolving in between.
You used to wonder
If this is how it would be
Every night of your life,
And if like your parents
You would grow accustomed
To the protean darkness.
They always went on
With their nightly tasks,
Unaware how the house had gotten larger,
How you were trapped in that high tower
Waiting for morning to restore
The familiar boundaries of the room.
Sometimes they would hear you crying
And would run up the stairs,
Rushing to your bedside
Where they waited with arms outstretched.
Never seeming to realize
How far you would have to fall.

STRANGE MUSIC BY THE WATER'S BOUNDARY

Not you brother,
Nor I.

Not dust,
Or the mere easy song of letting go.

Not the city's restless chatter,
The morning bird's gracious cry.

But something more like the ocean:
Ancient, Consuming, Depths Unnumbered.

That is the music we must remember.
A fierce, amoral tune

Ballooning up out of nothing,
Touching the charcoal night

With nameless notes and fringes,
Filling our cracked, coated bodies

With singing tones of gray.

CERTAINTIES

It's the face that changes first.
The mirror's long practice of recognition
Suddenly forgotten.

Then the hands, feeling as though they stretch
Miles from your body.

How dutifully the organ ages.
How sure the story takes a turn.

Transformation has its start
Where the plot seems most static.

The crossroads which you swore you would never travel
Find you one day on your journey home.

What you thought was furthest from your life
Comes and greets you at the door.

NOTATIONS

Woke up with a hurt larger than my body.
Must have been a dream.
Some late, dark thought
Whose content evades me.
I have always traveled in sleep
Through the interior of some desert region.
Have always taken charred, black debris
And smeared it across my face.
Such savage moments come up
From that other place inside.
Such god-like, terribly wondrous visions
Always gnawing in the night
At whoever in us does not want to break.

MANIFESTO

The share of duty is divvied amongst the heart.
Each of us indebted to the earth
Must give, just once, our suffering hands.
The world does not need redemption,
The tyrannical howling from below,
But just each miniscule part
To plant its one entrusted seed.
We die and the failure to live
Lingers on in regret,
A ravenous heat that eats through generations.
But to have met even for a moment
Our Star's singular calling
Urges the sleepy streets to waken.
The light which gives awareness
Needs only a crack to fill the room.

DELUGE

For love of something I could not name
I went out, disregarding the downpour.
My body was soaked to every cell
And I felt those tiny, essential ghosts
Sopping unhappily inside me.
The streets glimmered from the familiar mix
Of runoff and light,
Though even there the mysterious calling
Made the sequence strange.
As I traveled through the violent, unavoidable drifts
The water rose around me.
I found a small wooden boat tethered to a pole
And entered its single, narrow strip
Paddling for my life,
Refusing to turn away
Though I somehow knew that my house
Was impervious to flooding.
Lord, for whatever it is you put inside our bodies
That drives us out into the storm
I madly thank and praise you.
The reasonable life is an easy comfort.
It is better than that we drown
Of some great and stupid longing.

HOUSE

The wind, weary and acute, enters the keyhole
And settles in the opening between worlds.
A small spider taps its web into place
A hairsbreadth from the floor.
The inhabitants who signify
That something has been abandoned
Come uninvited, and you wonder
What it is you've lost.
The heart too is a house
Easily taken over by dust.
The flame stops sputtering
For a single moment
And before you know it
The drafty songs of autumn
Come creeping through the door.

IMAGINING IMMORTALITY

Deliberately, I give my body to the wind.
Surely the stone that thinks it is a bird
Will not be crushed by weather.
I imagine I am free from the threat of arrows,
From the thought that her and I
Will one day be apart beneath the furrows
Of the earth.
I'd give everything to sustain the magic,
To believe I'll be here forever
Happily in love on a bus ride home
While the rain hungrily dances at the window.
I'd give everything to press her to my body
And be assured that just this moment would last.

THE MAPLES & THE SEA

We seek in the maples a song
That will make us happy.
In the ocean too, on summer mornings,
When the surf is long and full of music.
Maybe somewhere a bird carries
The ultimate joy upon his back,
Dropping a few, flickering bits
Into any hand outstretched with bread.
Maybe one day when the water
Is exceptionally wild
A perfect happy thing
Will wash up from below.
And the people on the shore
Will smile unaccountably
As they stare puzzled at the sea.

FEAST

Perhaps it's like in the old myths.
Someone dies and they enter a cavernous realm
Where they confront whatever was left unsaid.
Or more luxuriantly, they return woven
Into magnolias and autumn leaves
Learning in utter peace the secret process.
Maybe they even come back renewed in language.
We say "sister" or "father"
And really mean the one who left us
Sneaking upon us in a song.
Maybe the dead are really just a bouquet
Of meaningful moments offered to decorate
The table at the unpredictable feast of memory.
Mysterious nectars that leave a troubling sweetness
In our mouths,
Though we are never really sure
If we ever touched them to our lips.

WEATHER IN OCTOBER

The white sky reminded the town
Of endless space.
It was a canvas inscribed with nothing.
An open realm where the birds
Flung an equal whiteness
In their dash against
The air.

The citizens upturned their gazes,
Wondering if at any moment
God would poke his head
From out amongst the absence.
Or even if a few stars would suddenly shine
In broad daylight,
Ablaze with inverse radiance.

It would only last an hour.
The normal clouds would come
Carrying messages of winter.
But still for a moment everyone felt
The immeasurable distance between us.
The abyss through which a few, creative gestures
Rise and fall in wonder.

REVISION

Imagine there is a bird
Lodged inside your heart,
A fire, treacherously burning in your ribs,
A dark, certain magic marrow-deep and singing.

Imagine too that we are music
Waiting to explode from our muffled lives,
To receive the cosmos in our bodies,
To pledge our songs against the deaf.

And listen then in the startling silence
For how you begin to dream,
For how the grass grows vibrant
In your mind.

Descartes led us deep into the house
Until we only believed in sealed doors.
From every entrance the earth is knocking.
The depths around us speak.

CONSECRATION

It intends nothing.
Whatever it is rustling in the grass.
A snail perhaps, winding his way along the earth,
A cricket leisurely stalking the light.
Or perhaps it's something more subtle,
The kind of thing that occasionally happens
Changing someone forever.
Though that was not its purpose.

One day the rain came unexpectedly
And a man who had never loved a thing
In his life
Felt the coating begin to crack.
He knelt down to touch the soil
And the first, inkling sadness
Entered through his palms.

LOOKING STARWARDS

It happens only a few times in a life.
The stars come out of their cosmic houses
And the sky turns ghostly with their light.
Suddenly the trees are wreathed in a wild radiance
And you almost feel that you can touch
The primitive blue of midnight
Burning overhead.
You walk the softly dampened streets
Where the mixture of loneliness and stars
Flares-up in plumes of phosphorous.
It happens only a few times
And always it speaks
To something beyond the comfort of our bodies,
To something not confined in bone.
A kaleidoscopic cell that can change and shift
With the auguries of the rain
Or the nearby sadness of the neighbor's cello.
Something so completely removed
From the laundry and yard work
That you lay down astonished.
Certain that though it is winter here,
It must be springtime in the stars.

A FEW WORDS ABOUT HAPPINESS & GRIEF

Two burning stones
Plunged from outer space
Into cold, autumnal water.
Their heavenly flame
Parting the depths
Deeper and deeper.

LEARNING ABOUT OPENNESS

To leave so much unbroken:
The calm plains of starlight
Unrent by morning,
The dew-soaked dresses of the grass
Neither dried nor tattered.
There is no lion here.
No hunger great or small.
The poem does not need
The images offered.
It can happily exist
Unreadable, in empty space.
But still it lets the world enter.
Relishes without attachment
The mist and moonshine,
The garden's deathly stillness,
The way someone looks out their window
And begins to ache.
It is a friend to them all.
But equally loves
The rich, erratic sound
Of the city readying to rise.

HOW IT MAY BE

Maybe you will make a pilgrimage
After years lost to the task at hand.
Will jump the fence line
With just a knapsack, a heart
And the labyrinth of darkness before you.
Suddenly you won't need utensils!
Will eat on your hands and knees
The dirty bread of the blessed.
You'll look like a beggar,
Disgusting to everyone around you.
You won't even own a car.
Only two shirts, and one in tatters.
Maybe you'll spend an entire evening
Crying beneath the stars.
Their inexplicable fire the only friend
To guide you.
Maybe you'll learn to speak
The one gnarled word the forest dreams of.
Learn how surely birdsong sings of death.
Maybe after years of restless wanting
You'll lay down in the supernatural fields
And hear, for the first time, the wheat around you.

THANK-YOU NOTE

Every night we borrow a dream
From the great and lovely mind
Of the world,
Dip our hands into the depths
To scoop a few shimmering drops
From its endless wellspring.

We say, "May tonight's journey be
Full of grace, its sunsets infinite,
Its birds happy with song.
May no friends leave us."

And the world mind, always vigilant,
Always keen to something beyond
Our knowledge, sends us deep into the dark,
Into volcanoes and caverns
Where our hearts must surely break.

And this is wise, though we are not sure why.
And this is wise.

PAEAN

Inside me, dreams drip and slide like sweat.
A life flourishes and ends on cue.
Such happy animals we are laying out alone
Mid-morning in the fog,
The craven appetite paused for a brief moment
With the sun.
Let's worship the early crickets praying in the dawn.
Let's worship the cat's long stretch against the earth.
I write a poem on the turned cheek of darkness.
I stroke the untroubled bodies of the grass.
The sea is far but its music finds me
For tiny intervals upon the wind.
The universe is large but I reel in my modest
House of bones, in love with the whole damn tapestry
Of gases, and lights, and stars.

ADVICE TO PEOPLE WHO SHUT THEIR DOORS AT SUNDOWN

It might be good to crawl
On your hands and knees
Through the spaces of the night,
To get down with the insular darkness,
Combing the virtuous grass
For those tiny nocturnal lives
Accompanying our own.
It might be good to test your voice
Against the humming web
Whose constant music
Rattles the leaves around you,
The bark-fall underfoot.
Perhaps you should open your door,
Step-out from your well-lit refuge,
Count yourself amongst the many nameless beings
Who populate your lawn.
You are a guest in their wild village.
Be gracious. Open your arms.
Let the crickets invite you in.

POSTLUDE

Do you hear the cosmos opening?
Its voice is like your voice,
Unsettling in the dark,
But somehow, still marvelously yours.
I think we must share a common music
With everything above us and below,
And if sometimes we may hear
A faint stirring in the grass
Perhaps we should not fear
A ghost beside us
But only press our bodies
Closer to the earth.
We must listen not for the slogans
Of a blind and dissonant city
But lean slowly and cautiously into the light.
We do not want to miss whatever song
Has waited for our coming.

ABOUT THE AUTHOR

Seth Jani is a poet, performer and publisher, as well as the founder and editor of Seven Circlepress.

He spent his youth in the mountains of Western Maine but has since traveled the country, living and working in places as varied as the forests of Vermont, California's Mojave Desert, The Big Easy, and currently the Pacific Northwest.
During these travels he has worked with various Conservation/Restoration non-profits as well as done extensive campaign work for progressive political causes.

His work has appeared in random places throughout the independent literary scene and he has taken it upon himself to self-release an array of books and pamphlets.

He is open to any thoughts, questions, criticisms etc. and encourages you to contact him at seth.david.jani@gmail.com.

www.sethjani.com

ABOUT THE PRESS

Founded in 2008 by poet Seth Jani, SCP is an online, in-print and ephemera based micropress that seeks to vigorously promote and distribute the works of new and established authors.

It commits to no prescribed esthetic but has a strong inclination to view art as a means of promoting unity and meaningful interaction.

The heart of the press is its online literary journal CircleShow, and its home on the web can be found at www.sevencirclepress.com.